FATS

FATS

BY DR. ALVIN SILVERSTEIN, VIRGINIA SILVERSTEIN, AND ROBERT SILVERSTEIN

ILLUSTRATIONS BY ANNE CANEVARI GREEN
FOOD POWER!
THE MILLBROOK PRESS ■ BROOKFIELD, CONNECTICUT

Library of Congress Cataloging-in-Publication Data

Silverstein, Alvin.
Fats / by Alvin Silverstein, Virginia Silverstein, and
Robert Silverstein; illustrations by Anne Canevari Green.

p.   cm.—(Food power!)
Includes bibliographical references and index.
Summary: Describes fats and their function in our diet.
Includes a gram-calorie chart and experiments.
ISBN 1-56294-208-5 (lib. bdg.)
1. Fat—Juvenile literature.   2. Lipids in human nutrition
—Juvenile literature.   [1. Fat.]   I. Silverstein, Virginia B.
II. Silverstein, Robert A.   III. Green, Anne Canevari, ill.
IV. Title.   V. Series: Silverstein, Alvin. Food power!
QP752.F3S55   1992
612.3′97—dc20   91-42169   CIP   AC

CONTENTS

YOUR BODY IS JUST LIKE A FACTORY

 FOOD IS THE **FUEL** THAT KEEPS YOUR FACTORY RUNNING.

 THE FACTORY USES MANY THINGS IN FOOD:
CARBOHYDRATES, **FATS**, **PROTEINS**, **VITAMINS**, **MINERALS**, AND **WATER** (WHICH HELPS COOL THE FACTORY AND CARRY THINGS AROUND IT).

 CARBOHYDRATES (SUGARS AND STARCHES) ARE THE FURNACE — THEY PROVIDE ENERGY.

 FATS ARE THE STORAGE DEPARTMENT: THEY STORE ENERGY FROM FOOD AND ALSO CARRY VITAMINS AROUND THE FACTORY.

 PROTEINS ARE THE BUILDING BLOCKS THAT ARE USED TO REPAIR AND ENLARGE THE FACTORY.

 VITAMINS HELP TO RELEASE THE ENERGY FROM FATS, PROTEINS, AND CARBOHYDRATES.

 MINERALS ARE THE CARPENTERS — THEY HELP TO BUILD BONES AND TEETH.

WHEN ALL FOOD IS COMPLETELY DIGESTED, WHATEVER ISN'T USED OR STORED LEAVES THE FACTORY AS **WASTE**.

WHAT ARE FATS?

Can you imagine eating a whole quarter pound of butter? That's how much fat the average American eats *each day*! It's no wonder most people these days think of "fat" as something bad, and supermarkets sell "low-fat" and even "fat-free" foods.

But we couldn't be healthy if we didn't eat *any* fat at all. The fats we eat contain vitamins and other key nutrients needed by the body. Fats are a rich source of energy, and they are also used to build nerves and the membranes surrounding cells. Fatty tissue helps to protect many organs of the body. Fats can be stored by the body for future needs or converted to other important chemicals. In fact, fats are one of the three major kinds of nutrients in foods that are used by the body for energy.

Fats also help to give foods a smooth, rich taste.

Scientists call fatty substances *lipids*. Strictly speaking, fats are lipids that are solid at room temperature; the liquid lipids are called oils. However, even so-called solid fats are usually rather soft, with a slick, greasy feel.

THE WORLD OF LIPIDS

When you hear the word "fat," the first thing you think of is probably the white fatty layer around the outside of a steak or chop. This is one of the most common kinds of fat. But there are a number of other kinds as well.

Different Kinds of Fats

The fat on a steak is an example of a *glyceride*. More than 90 percent of the fats found in nature are glycerides. Scientists call glycerides *simple lipids* because they contain only three elements: carbon, hydrogen, and oxygen. There are also a number of *compound lipids*, in which the fatty substances are combined with something else. The lipids also include some fatlike substances, such as cholesterol and vitamin D.

A Concentrated Energy Source

In proteins and carbohydrates, the elements carbon, hydrogen, and oxygen are combined into fairly small chemical units. These units are joined into chains, like beads on a string. In lipids, though, there is less oxygen, and the

same elements are combined in a different way, resulting in some important differences.

First of all, lipids can store a great deal of energy—over twice as much as proteins or carbohydrates can. This stored chemical energy (which is measured in calories) can be released in reactions with oxygen from the air. That is what happens in a fire, too, but the reactions in the body are more controlled. The energy they release may be used to power the body's activities, such as the movements of muscles or the chemical reactions that help us to see light or digest our food.

Glycerides

Glycerides are made up of a type of alcohol called *glycerol* and one or more *fatty acids.* A glycerol molecule has three places where fatty acids can attach. If a fat has a single fatty acid, it is called a *monoglyceride.* Two fatty acids attached to the glycerol molecule form a *diglyceride. Triglycerides* are formed when there are three fatty acids in each molecule of fat. More than 90 percent of the fats in our food are triglycerides.

Fatty Acid Chains

A fatty acid is a chain of carbon atoms with hydrogen atoms attached to it, plus an "acid" group. The acid group, which contains carbon, hydrogen, and oxygen atoms, reacts easily with other chemicals. For example, it combines with glycerol to form glycerides.

Some fatty acid chains have only a few carbon atoms. Others have as many as 20 or more. Lipids containing short-chain fatty acids are liquid oils, while those with long chains are usually solid fats.

Babies can digest short-chain fatty acids more easily than longer ones. Guess what kind of fatty acids are found in milk? (In fact, milk fat contains more short-chain fatty acids than other fats and oils do.)

The most common fatty acids in foods contain 18 carbon atoms. These acids include *oleic acid*, found in olive oil and other plant and animal lipids; *stearic acid*, the main fatty acid in beef fat; and *linoleic* and *linolenic acids*, which are sometimes called essential fatty acids because our bodies can't make them. (These are the only fatty acids we need to get from the foods we eat.)

Saturated and Unsaturated Fatty Acids

Fatty acids come in three types: *saturated*, *monounsaturated*, and *polyunsaturated*. The word *saturated* means that something is full, holding all that it can. The carbon atoms in a saturated fatty acid chain are holding all the hydrogen atoms they can. The bonds between the carbon atoms are very strong and not easily broken. An *unsaturated* compound, though, has fewer hydrogen atoms and contains what chemists call double bonds. These bonds are "hot spots" that can react fairly easily with oxygen molecules from the air. A monounsaturated fatty acid has one double bond, while a polyunsaturated fatty acid has two or more double bonds.

Saturated fats are found mostly in animal products such as meat and cheese. But all animal fats—including the lipids in your body—contain some unsaturated fatty acids as well. The oils in plant seeds are usually monounsaturated or polyunsaturated. As we'll see later, saturated fats are much less healthy for us than polyunsaturated or monounsaturated fats.

IT WAS A FRAMEUP – I WAS HYDROGENATED!

Check the label on a package of margarine or a jar of peanut butter. Do you see the word "hydrogenated" or "hardened"? This means that hydrogen atoms have been added to the double bonds in the unsaturated fatty acids. The chemical reaction is called *hydrogenation*. It is also referred to as *hardening* because the liquid oils are changed into solid fats.

Why do food manufacturers hydrogenate oils? To make them solid, so they can be spread on bread or crackers, and also to protect them from going bad. Remember, double bonds are very reactive. When they react with oxygen from the air, they form new compounds, which may taste or smell bad. Then we say the oil is "spoiled" or "rancid."

Another way to protect unsaturated fats from spoiling is to add an *antioxidant*, a chemical that protects foods

---

Turning good fats into bad

When polyunsaturated fats are hydrogenated to make them more firm, they become more saturated. Thus, margarines and other products containing hydrogenated vegetable oils may actually have as much saturated fat as butter. Hydrogenation can also change some polyunsaturated fatty acids to unnatural forms called "trans" fatty acids, which some health experts think may not be good for us. So hydrogenation makes oils more convenient to use, but it may decrease their food value.

Oil and water don't mix

If you try to mix oil and water together, you will find that they soon separate, forming two layers. The oil layer is always on top, because the oil is lighter than water. The two liquids seem to mix if you shake up the container, but soon you can see tiny oil droplets separating. They come together quickly, forming bigger and bigger globules until there is a solid oil layer on top again.

There is a way to keep oil and water mixtures from separating: by adding a chemical that has a fatlike part and a water-soluble part. You can see for yourself by adding a teaspoon of dishwashing detergent to a mixture of oil and water in a jar and shaking vigorously. A stable mixture called an *emulsion* is formed. Food manufacturers use edible chemicals to keep mayonnaise and other food emulsions from separating.

from the action of oxygen in the air. The additives BHT and BHA are antioxidants listed on the labels of many products containing fats and oils, such as cookies. Vitamin E, found in many fats and oils, is a natural antioxidant.

Other Lipids

You've probably heard about *cholesterol*. Most people think of it as something bad. True, it is part of the fatty deposits that may form inside arteries and lead to heart disease. But cholesterol isn't all bad. In fact, it is very important. It is found in nearly every tissue in the body.

Cholesterol can be found in many meats and other animal food products. But we don't really need to eat cholesterol in a healthy diet. The liver makes as much as we need.

Cholesterol is neither a glyceride nor a fatty acid. Instead, it is a steroid. Some of its carbon atoms are linked together like a tiny Tinkertoy, to form interlocking rings. All steroids contain this ring system.

Lipoproteins are combinations of a protein and a lipid. They help to carry fatty substances around in the bloodstream. (Their lipid part holds on to the fat, and their protein part dissolves in the watery blood.) The lipoproteins *HDL*, *LDL*, and *VLDL* are often called "good cholesterol" and "bad cholesterol." HDLs (the good cholesterol) carry cholesterol to the liver, where it is changed into bile salts and eventually sent out of the body. LDLs and VLDLs carry cholesterol through the bloodstream to the body cells. But if there is too much cholesterol, some of it may form fatty deposits in the artery walls and block the blood flow. Doctors do blood tests for LDL and HDL cholesterol to get an idea of people's heart disease risks.

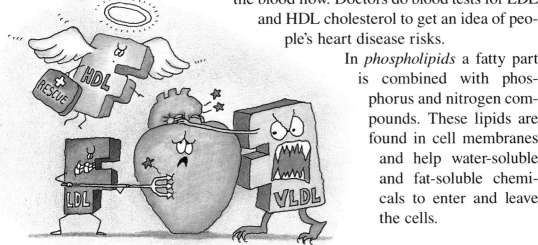

In *phospholipids* a fatty part is combined with phosphorus and nitrogen compounds. These lipids are found in cell membranes and help water-soluble and fat-soluble chemicals to enter and leave the cells.

FATS IN FOODS

How much fat do you eat? If you're like most Americans, it's probably more than you think. You may know that the butter you spread on your bread is mostly fat. So is the oil in salad dressing, the layer of fat around a steak or chop, or the white parts in a slice of bacon. But there are a lot of hidden fats in foods, too. You might cut off all the fat you can see on a slice of meat, but there is still a lot of fat that you don't notice, mixed in with the red meat fibers. Even after cooking, for example, nearly two thirds of the calories in a hamburger come from fat. Cheeses and nuts are high-fat foods, too. In fact, many of the foods that are good sources of proteins have large amounts of fat along with them.

Kinds of Fats

The fats in foods contain a variety of lipids, but most of them are triglycerides. A glass of whole milk, for example, contains 8.2 grams of fat, but only 33 milligrams (.033 of a gram) of that amount is cholesterol; triglycerides make up the rest. A few foods, though, are especially high in cholesterol. The 5.6 grams of fat in an egg yolk, for instance, includes about 230 milligrams of cholesterol; and a portion of beef liver contains 389 milligrams of cholesterol in just 4.9 grams of fat. (Vegetables, fruits, and grain foods, remember, contain practically no cholesterol.)

The various kinds of fats in foods contain an average of about 4,000 calories of stored energy per pound. One tablespoon of fat or oil has about 100 calories.

Of the three major nutrients, fats are the most concentrated energy sources. One gram of fat contains about 9 calories of energy. (One gram of protein or carbohydrate contains only 4 calories.)

Health experts say fats should account for about 30 to 40 percent of a child's diet, and no more than 30 percent of an adult's. They are talking about *calories*, not the weight or volume of the food. Package labels usually give the amounts of protein, carbohydrate, and fat per portion in grams. But the percentage of fat calories is easy to figure out. Just multiply the fat grams by 9, divide that answer by the total calories per portion, and multiply by 100.

Do We Need Fats in Foods?

Are fats really a necessary part of our diet, or just something that happens to come along with other, more useful nutrients? We might be better off eating less fat than we do, but do we need *any* fat? The answer is yes!

Fat provides essential nutrients. Our bodies can make most of the raw materials needed to build our body lipids. But foods such as corn oil, safflower oil, soybean oil, and some animal products supply essential fatty acids. We need only about the amount of polyunsaturated fatty acids in a tablespoon of vegetable oil each day. Unfortunately, most people eat much more than that.

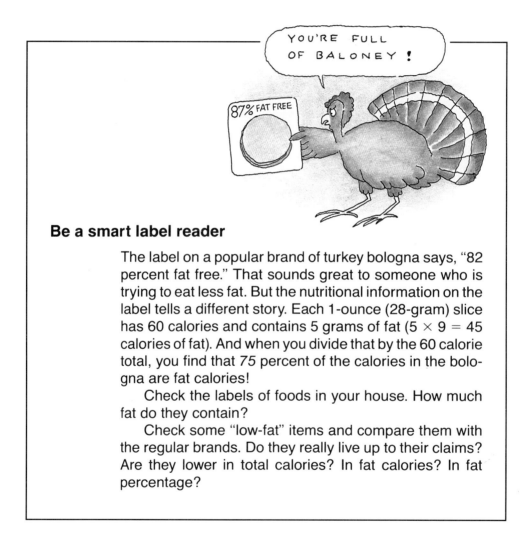

Be a smart label reader

The label on a popular brand of turkey bologna says, "82 percent fat free." That sounds great to someone who is trying to eat less fat. But the nutritional information on the label tells a different story. Each 1-ounce (28-gram) slice has 60 calories and contains 5 grams of fat (5 × 9 = 45 calories of fat). And when you divide that by the 60 calorie total, you find that *75 percent* of the calories in the bologna are fat calories!

Check the labels of foods in your house. How much fat do they contain?

Check some "low-fat" items and compare them with the regular brands. Do they really live up to their claims? Are they lower in total calories? In fat calories? In fat percentage?

Fats help transport fat-soluble vitamins into the body. Vitamins A, D, E, and K are not water soluble. Fats carry them into the body, and extra amounts of these vitamins are stored in the body fat.

Fats make us feel satisfied longer after a meal. They are digested more slowly than other nutrients. So the stomach and intestines stay full longer and don't send out hunger signals so soon after a fat-rich meal.

Fats taste good. The fats in foods make them taste and smell better to most people, and fatty foods feel smoother, juicier, and more tender. This is why we add fat-rich butter, margarine, salad dressing, coffee creamers, icings, and whipped toppings to other foods.

The average American eats 100 to 150 grams of fat each day. More than 60 percent of it is hidden in foods that we may not even suspect were high in fat.

What Foods Contain Fat?

One government survey of the foods Americans eat found that 39 percent of the fat came from meat, poultry, fish, and eggs; 11 percent from dairy products; 4 percent from nuts and dry beans; and 3 percent from flour, cereal, fruits, vegetables, and other foods. But guess what the largest single source of fats in our diet was? Fats *added* to foods during their preparation—butter or oil, for example—made up 43 percent of the total fat calories.

It's hard to believe how many calories the added fats contribute. A baked potato (without the skin) has about 145 calories. Add a tablespoon of butter, and you're adding another 108 calories. Eat a portion of french fries weighing the same number of grams as a baked potato, and you have 475 calories. And the same weight in potato chips would give you 825 calories!

Testing for fats

Take a brown paper bag and cut out a piece about 2 inches square. Rub a little butter on it. Does the butter leave a grease spot? That's a sign that fat is present. (If you hold the paper up to the light, some of the light will shine through.)

Try the same experiment with other foods. Give the paper time to dry thoroughly before you decide whether the test was positive or negative. Many foods contain water, and a water spot might look like a grease spot if it is still wet. But a real grease spot won't dry up and disappear, no matter how long you wait.

WHAT HAPPENS TO THE FOOD YOU EAT?

The organs of the digestive system are like work areas in a factory. Step by step, they prepare food for digestion, break down the nutrients into forms the body can use, and get rid of waste products.

Chewing and the warmth of the body help to soften the fats in foods and prepare them for digestion. Only a small part of the food lipids are digested by an enzyme in the stomach. Though the stomach acid is quite strong, it doesn't act on lipids.

In the small intestine, churning movements help to break down lumps of fat into tiny globules. Bile emulsifies these fat globules, keeping them suspended in the soupy mixture. Bile is made in the liver and stored in the baglike

Are fats hard to digest?

Not really, but fat digestion does take a long time. If you have diarrhea or are taking laxatives, the food moves through your intestines too quickly for the fats to be digested completely.

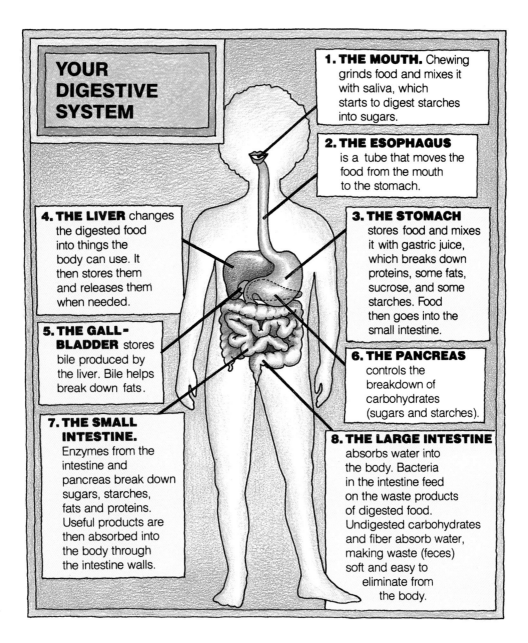

YOUR DIGESTIVE SYSTEM

1. THE MOUTH. Chewing grinds food and mixes it with saliva, which starts to digest starches into sugars.

2. THE ESOPHAGUS is a tube that moves the food from the mouth to the stomach.

3. THE STOMACH stores food and mixes it with gastric juice, which breaks down proteins, some fats, sucrose, and some starches. Food then goes into the small intestine.

4. THE LIVER changes the digested food into things the body can use. It then stores them and releases them when needed.

5. THE GALL-BLADDER stores bile produced by the liver. Bile helps break down fats.

6. THE PANCREAS controls the breakdown of carbohydrates (sugars and starches).

7. THE SMALL INTESTINE. Enzymes from the intestine and pancreas break down sugars, starches, fats and proteins. Useful products are then absorbed into the body through the intestine walls.

8. THE LARGE INTESTINE absorbs water into the body. Bacteria in the intestine feed on the waste products of digested food. Undigested carbohydrates and fiber absorb water, making waste (feces) soft and easy to eliminate from the body.

23)

gallbladder until a hormone from the small intestine signals that fatty food is waiting to be digested.

Both the pancreas and the small intestine produce enzymes that split triglycerides into diglycerides and monoglycerides, then into fatty acids and glycerol. These building blocks are put back together combined with proteins to form *chylomicrons,* which pass into the lymph.

THE BODY LIPIDS

Today most Americans eat three meals a day and may have several snacks as well. But our ancestors of long ago couldn't just go to the supermarket when there was nothing to eat. They had to hunt for or gather their food. When the hunting was good, or there were plenty of fruits or vegetables to pick, there was plenty to eat—more than they really needed. But they didn't have refrigerators. So if they tried to store a lot of food for later times, it would soon spoil. Instead, Stone Age people stored extra food in their bodies, in the form of fat.

Animals and plants use lipids to store energy, too. That is where the fats we eat come from. But our bodies can also change other nutrients into lipids. We can make fat from carbohydrates or proteins. Any extra nutrients we eat are stored away as fat, mainly triglycerides.

Where the Body Stores Fat

Fat can be stored in any cell in the body, but most of it is put into special cells called *adipose cells*, or *fat cells.* An adipose cell looks like an ordinary body cell when it is empty. But as fat droplets are packed into it, this cell bulges out. An adipose cell really looks fat when it is full!

Fat cells are grouped together to form *adipose tissue.* The thick layer of yellowish fat that we trim off a steak or roast is adipose tissue. Some people have more body fat than others. Usually, women's bodies store more fat than men's. The average man's body is 12 to 16 percent fat, and the average woman's is 20 to 25 percent fat.

Where the adipose tissue is found also varies from one person to another. In general, men tend to store fat around the middle of the body, in their abdomens. Women more often store fat in the hips, buttocks, and thighs. So a man's body with plenty of stored fat is shaped something like an apple, while a woman's body is shaped more like a pear.

How the body uses its stored fat reserves

When the body needs energy from its reserves, some of the stored triglycerides in the fat cells are broken down into free fatty acids. These fatty acids are carried in the blood to the various body cells that need energy.

Structures called *mitochondria* are the "power-houses of the cells." Inside them, fatty acids are combined with oxygen to release their stored energy. Chemical reactions break down the long carbon chains bit by bit, producing energy at each step.

Fat can also be stored in other areas. Muscles, for example, usually store the carbohydrate glycogen for a quick energy source, but they may also contain some adipose tissue. The "marbled" areas you can see in a steak are a combination of whitish adipose tissue and red muscle fibers.

Other Uses for Body Lipids

Cholesterol and phospholipids are important parts of cell membranes and nerve coverings. In addition to helping control what moves into and out of the cells, phospholipids and substances made from them also help in blood clotting and the transmission of messages from one nerve cell to another. Cholesterol helps to lubricate the skin and hair, keeping them from drying out. It is used in making steroid hormones that control the development of the body and many of its internal activities. It is also used to form vitamin D, which helps in the formation of strong, healthy bones and teeth. Cholesterol in bile aids in the digestion of food fats.

Prostaglandins, formed from the fatty acid called arachidonic acid, are another important part of cell membranes. They also act very much like hormones, helping to regulate the body temperature, blood pressure, acid production in the stomach, and many other body processes.

About half of the adipose tissue in a person of normal weight is found in the *subcutaneous fat*, which is just under the skin. This layer of fat acts like a blanket, keeping the body's own heat trapped inside and helping to keep us warm even when it is cold outside. The subcutaneous fat also acts as a cushion, protecting the skin and bones from getting bruised when there is pressure on them. Imagine how hard sitting would be if you didn't have soft pads of fat in your buttocks!

If half of the adipose tissue is subcutaneous fat, where is the other half? It is found in thick layers that support and protect internal organs such as the heart, kidney, and liver.

FATS AND YOUR HEALTH

Most people think fats are bad for them. But we have seen that our bodies do need some fat—just not as much as most people eat!

People are less active today, and thus we don't need as many calories as our ancestors did. Yet most of us still eat as much as—or even more than—people used to. And too much of what we eat is fat.

When too many of our food calories are fat calories, we harm ourselves in many ways. First of all, many fatty foods don't supply many vitamins and minerals, important nutrients that we need for good health. They also don't have much fiber, another needed food substance. But fatty foods make us feel full, and we may eat them instead of healthier foods, such as grains, fresh fruits, and vegetables. In addition, too much fat in the diet can cause many health problems.

Fat and Heart Disease

Many doctors feel a high-fat diet can lead to heart disease. It's not just the cholesterol in the food that's the problem. Eating large amounts of saturated fats may increase the amount of cholesterol in the blood—especially the "bad cholesterol," carried by LDLs. Some of this cholesterol may form fatty deposits, called *plaque*, in the linings of arteries. As the plaque deposits grow, the blood flow may be cut off. If this happens in the arteries bringing blood to the heart, a heart attack may result. If the blood supply to the brain is blocked, a stroke can occur.

Did you know . . .

Some people are more likely to develop *cardiovascular disease* (disease of the heart and blood vessels) than others. The differences seem to be hereditary. In some families, many members have heart attacks at a much younger age than usual. Blood tests show that they have unusually high levels of cholesterol, triglycerides, or both. Even the children of these families have high lipid levels.

Yet some people can eat a high-fat diet but still live a long and healthy life. This is true of Eskimos and Masai tribes in Africa, whose diet contains as much as 60 percent saturated fat. Studies have found that the people  who can eat large amounts of fats without getting heart disease tend to have larger than usual amounts of HDLs, the "good cholesterol." The same thing is true of carnivorous animals, such as cats, dogs, and seals. Their high HDL levels help to keep the fats in their meat diet from causing trouble.

The good news about heart disease is that the clogging of the arteries can be reversed. Decreasing the amount of fat and cholesterol in the diet helps to lower the amount of cholesterol in the blood. Replacing some of the saturated fats in the diet with unsaturated fats can help to bring down the amount of LDL cholesterol. A high-fiber diet also seems to lower the cholesterol in the blood and arteries. Exercise lowers the "bad cholesterol" and may even help to remove some of the plaque that has already formed. Over the last 30 years, Americans have been changing to healthier living habits like these, and there have been fewer deaths from heart and blood-vessel disease.

Fat and Cancer

There is a lot of evidence suggesting that a high-fat diet may lead to some forms of cancer. In the laboratory, animals fed low-fat diets develop fewer cancers than those fed high-fat diets.

Some scientists believe that polyunsaturated fats in foods may be converted to cancer-causing chemicals. Yet health experts recommend substituting these fats for some of the saturated fats in the diet to lower the risk of heart disease. What should we do? It is probably best to eat less of *all* fats, both saturated and unsaturated.

Dietary Fat and Obesity

The biggest fat-related health problem in the United States today is extreme overweight, or *obesity*. Experts believe that as many as 30 to 60 million Americans are obese. This includes almost one quarter of American children.

How do people get obese? Eating a lot of fats is one sure way to gain weight, because fat contains more stored energy than other nutrients. But remember that the body can also change any excess carbohydrates or proteins into stored fats. So obesity can also develop from eating too much of these.

Carrying around a load of excess fat puts a strain on the body. Obese people are more likely to develop ailments, including cancer, diabetes, arthritis, and heart disease.

But some people have a different problem. They're afraid of *looking* fat. In one poll, 90 percent of the people surveyed said they weighed too much, but only about 20 to 25 percent of Americans really are obese. Even young people have this problem. Some surveys have shown that many children as young as nine years old have already tried dieting!

Is Dieting OK?

Unsupervised dieting can be dangerous for anyone, but it is even more dangerous for young people, who need food for growing. Pound for pound, children need more fats than adults because their nerves, reproductive organs, and other important body structures are still forming. If you think you may be overweight, see a doctor to find out if you really are. And if you are, your doctor will show you how to cut down on the food you eat.

Americans spend $30 billion a year trying to lose weight. Most diets and gimmicks don't work, and any weight lost is soon gained back. Instead of trying fad diets or weight-loss gimmicks, the best plan for anyone of any age is to change poor eating habits into healthier ones. Learn to eat in moderation, eat many different kinds of foods, and eat less sugary and fatty foods.

Exercising is an important part of any plan for losing weight or maintaining a good weight. It uses energy and burns off calories. Health experts think the main cause of obesity in children is not getting enough exercise.

Many overweight children avoid competitive sports because they think people will make fun of them. But there are plenty of other ways to exercise, including riding a bicycle, walking, hiking, swimming, dancing, and skating.

47 calories per hour

71 calories per hour

118 calories per hour

235 calories per hour

OOF!

GRUNT!

330 calories per hour

TIPS FOR FAT-SMART EATING

A healthy diet is a good way of life for everyone, not just those who need to watch their weight.

Remember that fat is an important nutrient. Don't try to cut out all fat from your diet. Just cut down and, whenever you can, substitute polyunsaturated or monounsaturated fats for foods with saturated fats. Don't worry if you occasionally wind up eating more than 30 percent fat in one meal, or even in a day. If you splurge on an ice-cream sundae or some other high-fat treat, just be sure to eat some very low-fat meals over the next few days to balance things out.

Eating more vegetables and fruits and less dairy products and meat can cut calories and fat from your diet. Fruits and vegetables also contain fiber, which can help you feel full without adding calories. (Inside your stomach and intestines, fiber absorbs water and swells up to many times its original size, helping to make you feel full.)

What About Snacks?

Most experts think snacking is fine. In fact, many of them say that smaller, more frequent meals are better than the

2 TO 3 SERVINGS A DAY OF MILK, YOGURT, OR CHEESE

6 OR MORE SERVINGS OF ANY OF THESE PER DAY

2 OR MORE SERVINGS OF FRUIT A DAY

3 OR MORE SERVINGS OF VEGETABLES A DAY

2 TO 3 SERVINGS OF PROTEIN FOODS A DAY

large meals most of us eat. But snack on low-fat foods like fresh fruits, vegetables, or low-fat yogurt. Many snack foods, such as corn chips, potato chips, cookies, cakes, and pastries, contain fat as a main ingredient.

Peanut butter, seeds, and nuts are good protein sources, and many of their fats are polyunsaturated. But watch out! Nuts are high in fat calories, and it is easy to eat a lot of them because each one seems so small.

Fat-Cutting Tips

Oil, Spreads, and Condiments: Try eating bread or crackers without butter, and salad without the salad dressing. Or use just a dab of low- or no-calorie dressing.

Remember that margarine may contain unsaturated fats (unless it is hydrogenated), but it still has as many fat calories as butter.

A smart choice is to use vegetable oils instead of animal fats for cooking, or to use a nonstick spray on the pan instead. Remember that palm kernel oil and coconut oil contain saturated fats.

Meat, Poultry, and Fish: Eat meat less often. Substitute some meatless dishes with whole grains, legumes, and low-fat milk products as the source of protein. Meat can also be "stretched" by mixing it with vegetables in a casserole or grain products in a meat loaf.

How do they make low-calorie butter or margarine?

Butter and margarine contain 16 to 20 percent water. "Imitation margarine" has more water added, to lower the calories. "Whipped" butter or margarine has air whipped into it. The whipped products have the same number of calories per gram as regular spreads, but a smaller-weight portion can spread further.

Eat more fish and poultry, which have less saturated fats. The light meat of chicken or turkey has less fat than dark meat. And don't eat the skin—it contains nearly half of all the fat! Tuna packed in water contains much less fat than tuna packed in oil. Shrimp, lobster, and crab are higher in cholesterol than other seafood.

When eating meat, choose lean cuts and trim off the excess fat before cooking. Steaming, grilling, roasting, boiling, stewing, broiling, or baking on a rack to drain off the melted fat are healthier ways of cooking. Frying adds oil, and breading soaks up fat during frying.

Eggs: Eggs are a great source of protein, but a single egg yolk contains the entire amount of cholesterol the American Heart Association says we should eat in a whole day! Many experts recommend eating only three eggs per week. You can stretch the number of eggs you eat by using egg substitutes. Or you can cut down on cholesterol by getting rid of some of the yolks when preparing a meal. An omelet, pancakes, or French toast can be made with two whites and one yolk.

Dairy Products: A cup of whole milk contains about 8 grams of fat. Cheese has even more fat because it is concentrated. (It takes 20 cups of milk to make 1 pound of cheese.) Cheese and meat supply about the same amount of protein per weight, but cheese has a lot more fat.

Skim milk, with the fat removed, has only half as many calories as whole milk. So use low-fat dairy products, such as skim or low-fat milk, low-fat yogurt, part-skim ricotta and other cheeses, and ice milk.

Fat-Wise Eating

To cut down on fats, you'll need to pay attention to what you eat. Learn to check the ingredients on food packages.

Sometimes it seems hard to make smart food choices, especially when it comes to fats. High-fat foods are so tasty, and there are so many of them. But people have been getting more health conscious, and food manufacturers are getting the message. More prepared foods list ingredients on the label. There are many "low-fat" and "lite" substitutes for high-fat foods. Now there are even "no-fat" cakes, cookies, cheeses, ice cream, and salad dressings. Even fast-food restaurants offer lower-fat hamburgers and chicken. Although fat-smart eating requires some thought, it is getting easier all the time to enjoy the foods you like without eating too much fat.

(38

Do you know what you're eating?

How many total calories do these meals supply? What is the percentage of fat calories in each meal? (Use the chart of food values to figure it out.)

Orange juice, cornflakes with milk and banana, milk.

Bacon and eggs, toast (white bread), milk.

Peanut butter and jelly sandwich, milk.

Tuna salad with celery and salad dressing, lettuce and tomato, milk.

Hamburger on a bun with ketchup and onions, french fries, milkshake.

Steak, baked potato, green beans, lettuce and tomatoes, chocolate ice cream.

Baked cod, corn, broccoli, roll and butter, applesauce, milk.

Spaghetti with tomato sauce, eggplant, broccoli, peaches, tea.

Turkey with stuffing, cranberry sauce, sweet potatoes, peas, pumpkin pie, milk.

Eat right, exercise and get enough sleep. Your body needs your help to stay strong and healthy.

Nutritional Values of Common Foods

Food	Portion Size		Total Calories	Fats (g)	Fats (cal.)
Applesauce (sweetened)	1	cup	195	0.4	4
Bacon	3	pieces	109	9.4	85
Banana	1	banana	105	0.6	5
Broccoli (raw)	1	cup	24	0.4	4
Bun (hamburger)	1	bun	114	2.1	19
Butter	1	tablespoon	108	12.2	110
Cake (devil's food)	1	piece	227	11.3	102
Celery	½	cup	10	0.1	1
Cod (baked w/butter)	3½	ounces	132	3.0	27
Cookies (choc. chip)	2	cookies	99	4.4	40
Corn (cooked on cob)	1	ear	83	1.0	9
Cornflakes	1¼	cups	110	0.1	1
Cranberry sauce (jellied)	½	cup	209	0.2	2
Eggplant (boiled)	½	cup	13	0.1	1
Eggs (boiled)	1	large	79	5.6	50
French fries	10	fries	158	8.3	75
Green beans (boiled)	½	cup	22	0.2	2
Hamburger (broiled)	3½	ounces	289	20.7	186
Hot dog (beef)	1	frank	142	12.8	115
Ice cream (chocolate)	½	cup	280	17.0	153
Jelly	1	tablespoon	49	0.0	0
Ketchup	1	tablespoon	16	0.1	1
Lettuce (iceberg)	1	cup	7	0.0	0

Nutritional Values of Common Foods

Food	Portion Size		Total Calories	Fats (g)	Fats (cal.)
Milk (whole)	1	cup	150	8.2	74
Milkshake (chocolate)	1	cup	230	9.0	81
Onions (raw)	1/2	cup	27	0.2	2
Orange juice	1	cup	111	0.5	5
Peaches	1	peach	37	0.1	1
Peanut butter	1	tablespoon	95	8.2	74
Peas (boiled)	1/2	cup	67	0.2	2
Potato (baked w/peel)	1	potato	220	0.2	2
Pumpkin pie	1	piece	367	16.0	144
Roll (dinner)	1	roll	85	2.1	19
Salad dressing (mayo.)	1	tablespoon	58	5.0	45
Spaghetti	1	cup	155	0.7	6
Steak (sirloin)	3	ounces	240	15.0	135
Stuffing (bread)	1	cup	416	25.6	230
Sweet potatoes (baked)	1	potato	118	0.1	1
Tea	1	cup	2	0.0	0
Toast (white bread)	1	slice	64	0.9	8
Tomatoes	1	tomato	24	0.3	3
Tomato juice	1	cup	42	0.1	1
Tomato sauce	1/2	cup	37	0.2	2
Tuna (in water)	3	ounces	111	0.4	4
Tuna (in oil)	3	ounces	169	7.0	63
Turkey (light meat)	3 1/2	ounces	157	3.2	29

GLOSSARY

adipose cells—body cells that store fat.

antioxidant—a chemical that protects foods from the action of oxygen.

calorie—a unit measuring energy.

cardiovascular disease—diseases of the heart and blood vessels.

cholesterol—a fatlike substance that is both found in foods and made by the body.

chylomicron—a lipid found in the blood during the digestion and use of fats.

diglyceride—a glyceride containing two fatty acids.

emulsion—a stable mixture of tiny globules of two liquids that normally would form separate layers.

fatty acids—a part of a fat consisting of a chain of carbon and hydrogen atoms and an acid part.

glyceride—a simple lipid, containing only carbon, hydrogen, and oxygen.

glycerol—an alcohol that can combine with three fatty acids.

hardening—hydrogenation of unsaturated fatty acids, turning oils into fats.

hydrogenation—the addition of hydrogen to double bonds.

linoleic acid—an essential polyunsaturated fatty acid.

linolenic acid—an essential polyunsaturated fatty acid.

lipids—fatty substances, including fats and oils.

lipoproteins—combinations of a protein and a lipid.

mitochondria—structures in the cell where fatty acids are combined with oxygen to release their stored energy.

monoglyceride—a glyceride containing one fatty acid.

monounsaturated—containing one double bond.

obesity—extreme overweight.

oleic acid—a common monounsaturated fatty acid.

phospholipids—combinations of fat with phosphorous and nitrogen compounds.

plaque—fatty deposits in the arteries that may lead to a heart attack.

polyunsaturated—containing two or more double bonds.

prostaglandins—hormonelike chemicals formed from a fatty acid.

saturated fat—a fat whose carbon atoms hold all the hydrogen they can.

stearic acid—the main fatty acid in beef fat.

subcutaneous fat—adipose tissue just under the skin.

triglyceride— a glyceride containing three fatty acids.

unsaturated fat—a fat in which some carbon atoms are connected by double bonds, which can react with oxygen from the air.

FOR FURTHER READING

Cobb, Vicki. *More Science Experiments You Can Eat.* New York: Lippincott, 1979.

Cobb, Vicki. *Science Experiments You Can Eat.* New York: Lippincott, 1972.

O'Neill, Catherine. *How and Why: A Kid's Book About the Body.* Mount Vernon, N.Y.: Consumer Reports Books, 1988.

Ontario Science Center. *Foodworks.* Toronto: Kids Can Press, 1986.

Our Body: A Child's First Library of Learning. Alexandria, Va.: Time Life Books, 1988.

INDEX